D1123913

Adventurous
to
Zealous

All About Me from A to Z

Colleen Dolphin

Consulting Editor, Diane Craig, M.A./Reading Specialist

ABDO
Publishing Company

Published by ABDO Publishing Company, 8000 West 78th Street, Edina, Minnesota 55439. Copyright © 2009 by Abdo Consulting Group, Inc. International copyrights reserved in all countries. No part of this book may be reproduced in any form without written permission from the publisher. Super SandCastle™ is a trademark and logo of ABDO Publishing Company.

Printed in the United States.

Editor: Martha E. H. Rustad
Content Developer: Nancy Tuminelly
Cover and Interior Design and Production: Colleen Dolphin, Mighty Media
Photo Credits: BananaStock Ltd., Creatas, Shutterstock

Library of Congress Cataloging-in-Publication Data

Dolphin, Colleen, 1979-
   Adventurous to Zealous : all about me from A to Z / Colleen Dolphin.
      p. cm. -- (Let's learn A to Z)
   ISBN 978-1-60453-490-0
   1. Personality and emotions--Juvenile literature. I. Title.

   BF698.9.E45D65 2009
   155.2'32--dc22

                        2008023822

Super SandCastle™ books are created by a team of professional educators, reading specialists, and content developers around five essential components— phonemic awareness, phonics, vocabulary, text comprehension, and fluency— to assist young readers as they develop reading skills and strategies and increase their general knowledge. All books are written, reviewed, and leveled for guided reading, early reading intervention, and Accelerated Reader® programs for use in shared, guided, and independent reading and writing activities to support a balanced approach to literacy instruction.

About Super SandCastle™

Bigger Books for Emerging Readers Grades K-4

Created for library, classroom, and at-home use, Super SandCastle™ books support and engage young readers as they develop and build literacy skills and will increase their general knowledge about the world around them. Super SandCastle™ books are part of SandCastle™, the leading preK–3 imprint for emerging and beginning readers. Super SandCastle™ features a larger trim size for more reading fun.

Let Us Know

Super SandCastle™ would like to hear your stories about reading this book. What was your favorite page? Was there something hard that you needed help with? Share the ups and downs of learning to read. We want to hear from you! Send us an e-mail.

sandcastle@abdopublishing.com

Contact us for a complete list of SandCastle™, Super SandCastle™, and other nonfiction and fiction titles from ABDO Publishing Company.

www.abdopublishing.com • 8000 West 78th Street Edina, MN 55439 • 800-800-1312 • 952-831-1632 fax

This fun and informative series employs illustrated definitions to introduce emerging readers to an alphabet of words in various topic areas. Each page combines words with corresponding images and descriptive sentences to encourage learning and knowledge retention. AlphagalorZ inspires young readers to find out more about the subjects that most interest them!

The "Guess what?" feature expands the reading and learning experience by offering additional information and fascinating facts about specific words or concepts. The "More Words" section provides additional related A to Z vocabulary words that develop and increase reading comprehension.

These books are appropriate for library, classroom, and home use.

Aa

Guess what?

Make sure to be safe and tell an adult before going on an adventure.

Adventurous

An adventurous person tries new and exciting things.

Anxious

An anxious person worries about what will happen next.

Brave

A brave person is not afraid of a challenge.

Bossy

A bossy person tells other people what to do.

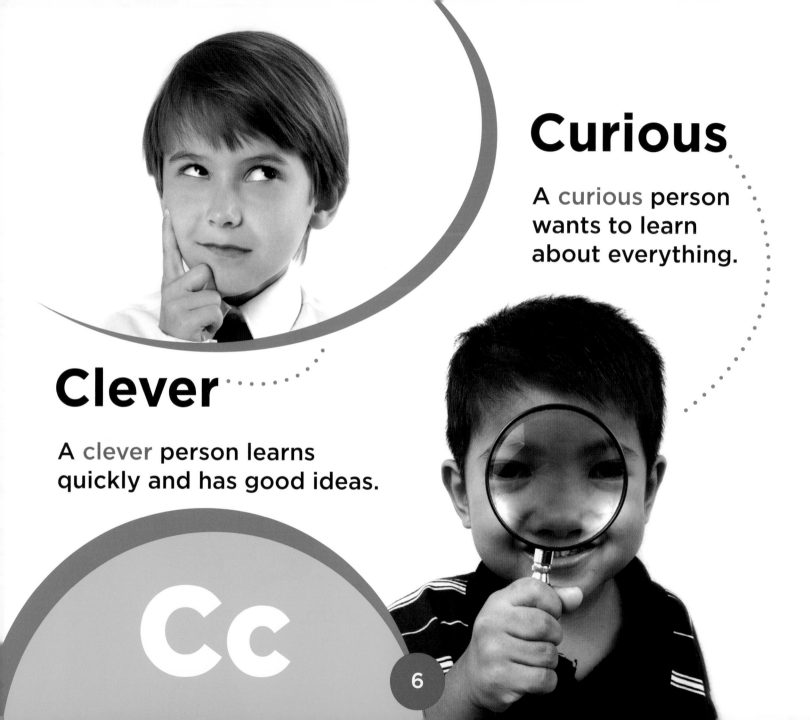

Curious

A curious person wants to learn about everything.

Clever

A clever person learns quickly and has good ideas.

Cc

Dependable

A dependable person
is someone who can
be trusted.

Daring

A daring person
likes to take chances.

7

Dd

Easy-Going

An easy-going person is relaxed.

Eloquent

An eloquent person can speak well.

Ee

8

Foolish

A foolish person
makes bad decisions.

Funny

A funny person
can make other
people laugh.

9

Gg

Generous

A **generous** person is giving and shares with others.

Gullible

A **gullible** person believes almost anything.

Honest

An honest person tells the truth.

Humble

A humble person does not like to brag.

Hh

11

Ii

Independent

An independent person can work or play alone.

Imaginative

An imaginative person has a very creative mind.

Jovial

A jovial person is happy.

Jj

Guess what?

A jealous person is sometimes called *green with envy*.

Jealous

A jealous person wants something that belongs to someone else.

13

Kind

A **kind** person is caring and likes to help others.

Knowledgeable

A **knowledgeable** person is wise and has learned many things.

Kk

Loyal

A loyal person is faithful and can be depended on.

Lazy

A lazy person does not like to work or do things that take effort.

Mature

A mature person thinks like an adult.

Mischievous

A mischievous person likes to cause trouble.

Mm

16

Guess what?

A person that causes trouble is called a *mischief-maker*.

Nervous

A nervous person is worried about many things.

Noisy

A noisy person is loud.

Nn

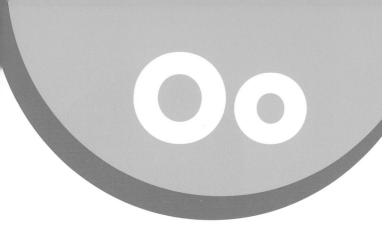

Obnoxious

An obnoxious person tries to get attention from other people.

Optimistic

An optimistic person expects good things to happen.

Picky

A picky person likes things to be a certain way.

Pessimistic

A pessimistic person expects bad things to happen.

Qq

Quick

A quick person can do things fast.

Quiet

A quiet person does not make a lot of noise.

Rude

A rude person has bad manners.

Guess what?

A person that gives respect usually gets respect.

Respectful

A respectful person is mannerly and cares about others.

21

Rr

Stubborn

A stubborn person does not change very often or listen to others.

Suspicious

A suspicious person does not trust other people.

Ss

22

Talkative

A talkative person likes to chat.

Tt

Thoughtful

A thoughtful person is considerate of others.

Unfriendly

An unfriendly person does not like being around other people.

Understanding

An understanding person is sympathetic and accepts other people.

Uu

24

Vibrant

A vibrant person is lively and has spirit.

Vulgar

A vulgar person says and does gross things.

Guess what..?

A vulgar person has very bad manners.

Vv

25

Ww

Whimsical

A whimsical person thinks of many fun and silly things to do.

Wise

A wise person knows many things and makes good decisions.

26

Xenomaniac

A xenomaniac is a person interested in other cultures.

Xenodochial

A xenodochial person is nice to strangers.

27

Yy

Youthful

A **youthful** person acts young no matter what his or her age is.

Guess what...?

A youthful person is also called *young-at-heart*.

You

What traits describe **you**?

28

Zealous

A zealous person is enthusiastic!

Zany

A zany person acts silly and clowns around.

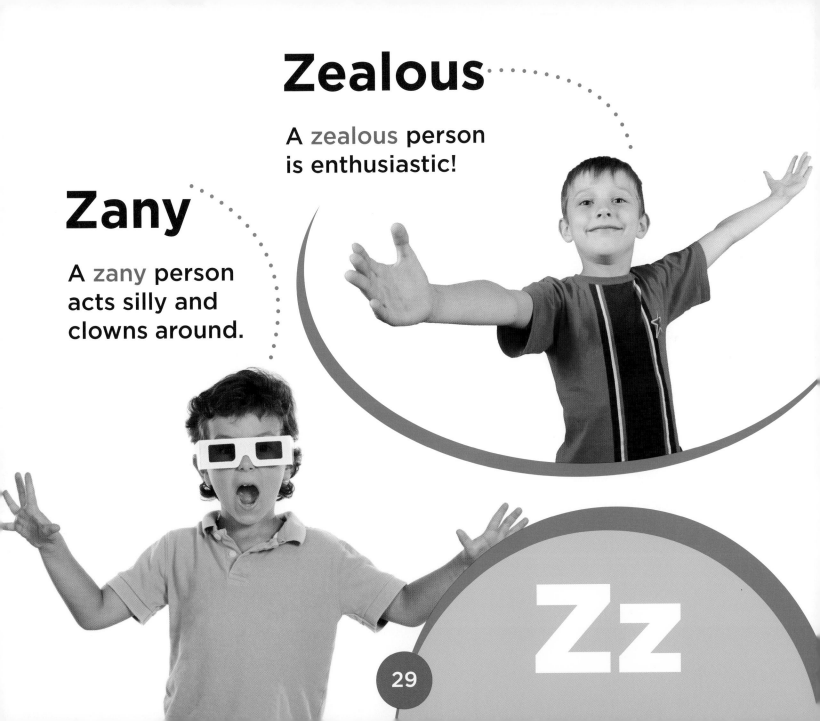

29

Zz

Glossary

attention – the act of concentrating on or giving careful thought to something.

brag – to talk about what one owns or can do in order to impress others.

challenge – a test of one's abilities in a tough and exciting situation.

chance – risk.

chat – to talk with someone.

considerate – aware of the feelings and needs of others.

creative – having unique ideas.

culture – the behavior, beliefs, art, and other products of a particular group of people.

decision – a choice.

effort – the work it takes to do something.

enthusiastic – showing great enjoyment or approval.

expect – to assume something is going to happen.

faithful – loyal.

lively – full of energy.

manners – polite behavior.

relaxed – being at rest or at ease.

stranger – an unfamiliar person.

sympathetic – to understand how someone else is feeling.

trait – a feature or quality that identifies someone or something.

trust – to rely on the character, ability, or strength of a person or thing.

vocabulary – all of the words known and used by someone.

More Personality Traits!

Can you learn about these personality traits too?

ambitious	fearless	pleasant
animated	finicky	polite
arrogant	gentle	proud
bewildered	giddy	reliable
blasé	gloomy	responsible
brilliant	greedy	rowdy
calm	grouchy	sarcastic
candid	happy	secretive
careful	harsh	selfish
confident	helpful	sensitive
confused	immature	silly
determined	lackadaisical	sincere
dishonest	lively	sly
doubtful	loving	smart
dutiful	mean	tense
eager	moody	trusting
efficient	mysterious	unruly
energetic	obedient	valiant
fair	peaceful	warm-hearted